HOW TO BE *HAKUNA MATATA*

HOW TO BE HAKUNA MATATA

ZEHA TEMBO

T

Troubador Publishing Ltd
Unit E2 Airfield Business Park
Harrison Road, Market Harborough
Leicestershire LE16 7UL
Tel: 0116 279 2299
Email: books@troubador.co.uk
Web: www.troubador.co.uk

ISBN 978 1 83628 052 1

British Library Cataloguing in Publication Data.
A catalogue record for this book is available from the British Library.

Printed and bound in Great Britain by 4edge Limited
Typeset in 11pt Minion Pro by Troubador Publishing Ltd, Leicester, UK

For my brother, who endured and dared to win
And for my mother, the constant wind beneath
my wings

CONTENTS

Chapter 1

ON BELIEVING IN YOURSELF

Mwanzo wa jino ufizi
A TOOTH BEGINS ITS GROWTH IN THE GUM

In the beginning, your plans may appear somewhat far-fetched to those that don't share your vision. Maintain your belief and self-confidence in your aspirations. The longer people call it a pipe dream, the more established your plans will become.

Mjanja wa usingizi ni yule aliyeamka
THE SLEEP EXPERT IS ONE WHO IS AWAKE

Going with the flow is for those that know when and where they plan to change direction. Listen to your intuition and dare to be the odd one out. Persist in asking 'why?' Success is not a dish commonly served with popular opinion.

Akuangushaye hukufunza kupigana
THOSE THAT KNOCK YOU DOWN TEACH YOU HOW TO FIGHT

A setback is a little dose of humility and at the same time the firelighter you need to see you through to the next round. It is exhausting to keep resisting people who wish to keep you where you are. Do not give in. Be your own cheerleader. For every closed door, there will be a window, a chimney or even a cat-flap. Oh, and try knocking on other doors too.

Atakae hachoki
A SEEKER DOES NOT GROW WEARY

Define 'made it' then multiply it by 10. That's the reward that awaits, if you persevere. Your efforts and hard work today will count as milestones of knowledge and experience. It's tough, it is relentless, energy sapping – so go ahead, cry. Take a break. When you've let it all out, pick yourself back up and try again.

Mzoea punda hapandi farasi
ONE WHO GETS INTO THE HABIT OF RIDING A DONKEY WILL NEVER RIDE A HORSE

Tear yourself away from your comfort zone. Ignore any negative thoughts of not being good enough, or clever enough, or too young or too old. Don't settle for less to comply with the norm. Be restless with a purpose and keep your hopes alive. Turn TikTok into tick-tock. 😊

Ajizi nyumba ya njaa
INDECISION IS THE DOORWAY TO AFFLICTION

If it seems like a good idea but you are not one hundred per cent sure, do it anyway and deal with the consequences as they unfold. Start today with a decisive action, tomorrow draw up a plan, the following day commit yourself, and the next day, nothing will stand in your way.

Dira ya binadamu ni kichwa
A PERSON'S COMPASS IS THEIR MIND

Where are you going?

La kwanza udhalili, la pili ukamilifu
FIRST HUMILITY, SECOND ACCOMPLISHMENT

Your mind is like an engine; it does not function when parts are missing. Identify your missing parts. Understand your vulnerabilities. Acknowledge your strengths and learn how to deal with your weaknesses. Then, find your path and be on your way.

Baada ya dhiki faraja
ADVERSITY GIVES WAY TO SUCCESS

For every success story, there's usually a

funny part where it all went wrong. Of course, it's only funny when retold at a later date. Today, face that challenge and try switching your focus from the odds to your goals. Grab every opportunity and if it rains, remember the sun is still shining behind the clouds.

Nyota haionekani mchana
STARS ARE NOT VISIBLE IN DAYLIGHT

There is something wonderful about being a gem. That's you. Wherever you are and whatever you are doing, you are exactly where your steps and mis-steps, a sprinkle of miracles and a slice of misfortunes have led you to be. Your status and circumstances may indeed change for the better, but you will find that you are still the same. As special then as you are today.

Leo kwako, kesho mwenziwe
TODAY BELONGS TO YOU, TOMORROW IT BELONGS TO YOUR NEIGHBOUR

When envy knocks on your door, as it sometimes will, open the door just a fraction to peep out, then shut the door and bolt it, firmly.

Taabu ya mtu ndiyo raha yake
A PERSON'S WORRY IS THEIR COMFORT

There is a wide disparity of means in the world. Whilst some people have problems; others encounter challenges. Problems strip one of the ability to think clearly. Challenges inspire ideas. What if the whole of the world's population were actively engaged in coming up with innovative solutions? Today, unfortunately, this is not possible because the majority of people lack basic needs. The United Nations lists 17 goals in the 2030 Agenda for Sustainable Development: A shared blueprint for peace and prosperity for people and the planet, now and into the future.

Follow, like, share: https://sdgs.un.org

Chapter 2

ON BUILDING CHARACTER

Chamlevi huliwa na mgema
A DRUNK'S FORTUNE IS THE BARTENDER'S FORTUNE

Addiction is very much like boarding a faulty aircraft to flee a war zone; this is a difficult and complex situation to deal with on your own. By all means try, but if you do not succeed you must seek professional help as soon as possible. Freedom will only be gained when you can say *no!* to your inner voice.

Heri kujikwaa kidole kuliko ulimi
IT IS BETTER TO TRIP OVER YOUR TOE THAN TO TRIP OVER YOUR TONGUE

When anger or resentment creeps in, it creeps out when you least expect it to. Thoughts turn into words, one way or another. Learn to discipline your thoughts by finding the good in others then spin a positive vibe. If no good can be found, at the very least try to form a balanced opinion.

Kupoteza njia ndiyo kujua njia
TO LOSE ONE'S WAY IS TO FIND ONE'S WAY
The world is an unforgiving place because time is a priceless commodity. If or when you make a mistake, expect and accept that you will have to pay the price. The price, though harsh, is also your secret superpower that will guide you to your next chapter. Your present is here, seize the opportunity.

Jina jema hungara gizani
A GOOD REPUTATION SHINES IN THE DARK
Everyone's mind has a storage filing system. One of the folders is reserved for esteemed people, respected for their principled, sincere character and commendable actions. No one can trick their way into that folder. You have to earn your place in it by doing the right thing. Once you're in, the credit is all yours.

Chumia juani ule kivulini
WITHSTAND THE SUN TO REST IN THE SHADE
Today every professional athlete in the world will know the exact countdown in

days, possibly even the hours, to the next Olympics. You too can start a training schedule for your very own personal best record-breaking goals. Adopt a mindset that will sustain any amount of effort by keeping your eyes on the prized medal.

Mlafi huuliwa na tamaa yake
A GLUTTON IS CONSUMED BY HIS OWN GREED

'I want more' turns into 'I want everything' in the blink of an eye. Such is human nature. Beware of the trap of trappings. In other words, make as much effort to pursue internal peace as you do to pursue external wealth. You will gradually build up a personal fortress filled with contentment and gratitude.

Mdumia kazi hakosi cha kumfaa
A DILIGENT WORKER CANNOT FAIL TO FIND A SUITABLE OCCUPATION

Work makes the world go round. So does love, but work has built up a bad press. For many, work is simply a means to pay the bills. It's true, is it not, that work is one of the few legacies that define one's life? What you do matters. How you do it can and does change the world.

Chuki humchoma anayeihifadhi
HATE BURNS WHOMEVER SHELTERS IT

Hate resembles a set of traffic lights. At the highest level, it is red and grinds you to a halt. No one goes anywhere, least of all you. When you start to let go, the lights turn to amber, and there is some hope for you. If you wish to move on, release the bitterness and the lights will turn green. It's all entirely up to you.

Mti upigwao na mawe in mti wenye matunda
THE TREE THAT BEARS FRUIT ATTRACTS STONES

Whatever your achievements are, you are bound to divide opinion. Productivity attracts attention, both good and bad. Keep on doing what you are doing, enjoy your success and ignore the noise.

Usipoziba ufa utenjenga ukuta
IF YOU DO NOT REPAIR A CRACK, YOU WILL BUILD A WALL

Life is harsh. Not only do you have to deal with the everyday challenges, but you also have to address those matters that are simply, easier to pack-away for another day. Yep, there are no trophies for looking the other way or for being in denial, no matter how good you are at it.

Asiye kubali kushindwa si mshindani
A LOSER IS NOT A WINNER DESPITE THEIR OBJECTIONS

That Hot Chocolate song about everyone being a winner speaks only to love affairs. You, me and everyone else every now and again will lose and are losers! L sign on my forehead at you. Let it hurt, it's your ego that hurts by the way. So, tame your ego and get over it.

La mnyonge huangushwa na upepo
LAZY DEEDS ARE BLOWN AWAY BY THE WIND

The visible and invisible barriers that you will face in life demand a strong character, a determined mind and a disciplined work ethic. Don't worry if you don't recognise any of these characteristics. Bring and present the very best of you seeking only the very best for yourself.

Mtu asiyejua aendako hana afikako
A PERSON WHO DOES NOT KNOW WHERE THEY ARE GOING GOES NOWHERE

A journalist once interviewed three athletes before the start of a race. He posed the same question to all three. 'What is your plan for today?' Athlete 1 confidently answered, 'I will try to win the race!'. Athlete 2 said, 'I will do my best to win the race'. Athlete 3, looking at the journalist, said, 'I am here to win the race'.

Shimo la ulimi mkono haufutiki
THE TONGUE LEAVES A GAP TOO WIDE TO BE COVERED BY THE HAND

Hurtful words have a crazy habit of sticking to the memory. As a matter of fact, so do genuine compliments. You have control over what you think, and by default what you say. Defend or offend. Change your thoughts, change the narrative.

Lila na fila hazitangamani
GOOD AND EVIL ARE NOT COMPATIBLE

A church priest once said, 'We want fire with our left hand and water with our right hand'. One hand is a champion of goodness, the other is our selfishness. They are both innate in every one of us. It's a daily battle. To win it, commit yourself to showing kindness.

Kawia ufike
SLOW DOWN TO ARRIVE

A job well done versus a rushed botch job. Frame the time pressure dilemma in this way and it is clear what everyone prefers.

Fuata nyuki ule asali
FOLLOW THE BEES TO EAT HONEY

Thanks to technology, finding your tribe these days is easy. Align yourself with people who share your ambitions or have had the vision to make it happen.

Mazingara ni chanzo cha kufuzu
ONE'S ENVIRONMENT IS THE GROUNDING FOR SUCCESS

The one sure and tested way to change your circumstances is to believe in your ability to succeed. Elevate your mindset, with a vow to escape – start planning today.

Tabia ni ngozi
HABIT IS SKIN

You are more likely to be associated with your one negative trait, despite having a whole host of positive traits. You probably think, I cannot change, it is my character! Could this be that it is 'your lack of character?' From the book *The Way*, by Josemaria Escrivá.

Mbaazi ikikosa maua husingizia jua
WHEN A SHRUB DOES NOT FLOWER, IT BLAMES THE SUN

When you admit responsibility, you begin the healing process within yourself. In life there will be other altogether different chances. This will be your opportunity to apply lessons learned and achieve those dreams.

Kila kufuli na ufunguo wake
EVERY PADLOCK HAS ITS KEY
1 in 8 billion

I am one in 8 billion
I am unlike anyone else

I do not look as good as others/
I LOOK AS GOOD AS I FEEL ABOUT MYSELF

I dislike my image in the mirror/
I LOOK MY BEST AND CARE ABOUT MY
APPEARANCE
I wish I was as popular/
I AM APPRECIATED

I wish I was as liked/
I AM RESPECTED

I wish I was as admired/
I AM NOT YET A PAINTING

I wish I was as loved/
I LOVE MYSELF

I wish I was as normal/
I AM PURPOSEFULLY DESIGNED

I am unlike anyone else
1 am one in 8 billion!

Chapter 3

ON OVERCOMING FAILURE

Heri kuliwa na simba huliko kuliwa na fisi

TIS MORE NOBLE TO BE EATEN BY A LION THAN BY A HYENA

You heard it here first, people! Fail BIG. Aim high, pursue those lofty goals and if you fall short, so be it. Approach opportunities with boldness and inner confidence. Well done for taking the risk.

Ngombe hailemewi na nunduye

A COW DOES NOT TIRE OF ITS HUMP

Not only have you failed, but the results are now on display for the whole world to see. This prayer by Reinhold Niebuhr is fitting: 'O God grant me the serenity to accept the things I cannot change; courage to change the things I can; and wisdom to know the difference'.

Atangaye na jua hujuwa

ONE WHO WANDERS WHILST THE SUN SHINES KNOWS

A setback affects first and foremost the belief system upon which ideas are built. You will doubt yourself. Be prepared to dig deep into your reserves to maintain some degree of rationality. Success is elusive, the ride is bumpy, keep moving.

Majuto ni mjukuu mwishowe huja kinyuma

REGRETS ARE LIKE A GRANDCHILD, THEY COME WITH THE PASSING OF TIME

Volcanologists are still trying to figure out the precise trigger mechanism effect between a quake and an eruption. In nature, every action leads to a reaction. And so it is that every little thing you do today will be of some meaning someday. Make it count.

Ngano ina ncha saba

A STORY HAS SEVEN ENDINGS

Why stop at your first defeat when it is just the beginning of many more on the road to success? So what if other people become impatient when you fail at something? All you need is a flexible mindset, grit determination and a wild imagination. Godspeed.

Mlilia nasibu hufa hali maskini
ONE WHO RELIES ON LUCK WILL DIE POOR

What's luck got do to with it? Yes, you may deserve a break. However, opportunities arise and are seized when they are met with preparedness. Go ahead and make your own luck.

Ushikwapo shikamana
WHEN YOU FIND YOURSELF IN A TIGHT SPOT, TIGHTEN YOUR GRIP

Do not let pride or embarrassment hinder your chances of recovery from a setback. Be open to asking and receiving assistance from those that are in a position to help you. Be precise about the support you need and do not expect unlimited free lunches.

Mpiga ngumi ukuta huumiza mkonowe
ONE WHO PUNCHES THE WALL INJURES HIS OWN FIST

Do not add insult to injury by reacting angrily at any sticky situation you happen to find yourself in. The more powerless you are, the more likely you are to experience feelings of frustration. Focus your efforts on Plan B.

Lipatalo hupishwa
LET WHAT HAS PASSED REMAIN IN THE PAST

You deserve a fresh start, every single day. Look, there's a green light up ahead.

Maji yakimwagika hayazoleki
SPILLED WATER CANNOT BE RESTORED

How universal this *methali* is! It's no use crying over spilled milk. It's a cautionary reminder that time is precious. The mind spends half of the time in the past, some of the time in the present and the rest of the time in the future. Rebalance your mind to win the race.

Mpanda ngazi hushuka
HE THAT CLIMBS THE LADDER COMES BACK DOWN

Be humble. There is a good reason to believe that one day you too might lose your status, but, more importantly, there is the simple recognition that each and every individual deserves equal respect.

Dawa ya moto ni moto
THE REMEDY OF FIRE IS FIRE

They also say: live by the sword, die by the sword. Do not rely on being lucky. Disengage from activities that will only result in your ruin. The pursuit for revenge is not akin to the pursuit for justice. Spare yourself from transforming from the victim into a villain.

Jana hairudi tena
YESTERDAY IS NOT COMING BACK

Time spent wishing for another chance is time spent ruining your day. Avoidable mistakes are disorienting as they strike at the very core of reasoning, allowing regret and shame to take over. Sticking to rewind will not change the outcome. Shift your thought patterns to what you could and should do today.

Mtaka yote hukosa yote
WHOEVER WANTS EVERYTHING LOSES EVERYTHING

Some people view acts of kindness as an act of weakness that should be taken advantage of. Fact. Are you one of those people who repay kindness with scorn? This one's for you. And yeah, speak to a therapist/counsellor/someone.

Jungu kuu halikosi ukoko
A COOKING POT WILL NOT MISS SOME CRUST

With the passage of time, one of the questions that is likely to arise is how best to deal with the weight of past mistakes. You know better. Do better. The benefit of physical activity or exercise, as a coping mechanism and mood booster should not be underestimated. Don't' despair.

Kilima uzuri mbali, karibu kina majuto
THE BEAUTY OF A MOUNTAIN IS FROM A DISTANCE; THE CLOSER YOU GET THE MORE THREATENING IT BECOMES

The horizon looks great and smells of sweet success.

PS: Take off those rose-tinted glasses and roll up your sleeves!

Ukiona vyaelea vimeundwa
A SHIP THAT SETS SAIL HAS BEEN BUILT

Success is only the end snippet of the whole story. Strive to see the whole picture. The correct question is, how long and what did it take? Take inspiration and be encouraged. The freedom and security that is gained from prosperity can be simply *magnifique!* No sweat, no glamour.

Chapter 4

ON FAMILY AND RELATIONSHIPS

Mla nawe hafi nawe ila mzaliwa nawe

FRIENDS DINE WITH YOU, FAMILY DIES WITH YOU

Social networks and followers have been known to disappear overnight. As you journey through life's seasons, don't forget that family remains a pillar that you can lean on, and the foundation from which you can bounce from.

Kupendana ni kuvumiliana

TO LOVE IS TO BEAR WITH ONE ANOTHER

'Love is patient, love is kind. It does not envy, it does not boast, it is not proud. It does not dishonour others, it is not self-seeking, it is not easily angered, it keeps no record of wrongs. Love does not delight in evil but rejoices with the truth. It always protects, always trusts, always hopes, always perseveres.' (1 Corinthians 13: 4-8).

Kuku havunji yai lake
A CHICKEN DOES NOT BREAK ITS OWN EGGS

Good parents nurture, protect and look after their own children, just as nature intended. The family unit at its best is the safest place to be.

Mtu na rafikiye ni kama kombe haziachi kuchakacha
FRIENDS ARE LIKE TEACUPS, ALWAYS CLINKING

Never allow a disagreement, get in the way of a good friendship.

Rafiki wa kweli ni tunu aali
A GOOD FRIEND IS A PRECIOUS TREASURE

Friendships are like a beautiful garden, vibrant and yet, tranquil. Allowing of critique every now and then, absorbing rain and sunshine with the changing seasons and blossom, when devoted time and attention.

Jirani ya karibu si ndugu wa mbali
A CLOSE NEIGHBOUR IS NOT THE SAME AS A DISTANT RELATIVE

Cherish those relationships that add to your practical well-being. They are just as important as those that you have labelled 'my friends'.

Vita vya panzi neema ya kunguru
A GRASSHOPPER'S FIGHT IS THE CROW'S DELIGHT

Don't assume that infighting between relatives has no clear winners or losers. Chances are that third parties are profiting from it.

Aliyekula kitovu chako, hatakuachia utumbo
WHOEVER NIBBLES AT YOUR NAVEL WILL TAKE YOUR INTESTINES OUT TOO!

Learn to choose your friends carefully. With every new relationship, start as you mean to go and always define your boundaries. Respond appropriately and promptly to interferences on your well-being.

Akufukuzaye hakwambii toka
A PERSON THAT WANTS TO GET RID OF YOU WILL NOT TELL YOU TO GET OUT

Take the hint. When people care about your feelings, they will seldom be as direct with you. Communication can be a wide array of actions. To preserve the relationship don't ignore the subtle cues.

Radhi ya baba na mama ni ufalme wa dunia
A PARENT'S BLESSING IS A WORLD OF FORTUNE

In African culture, there is a cohesive

bond that ties the older generation to the new generation. The backdrop is a well-trodden path of respect and obedience on the one hand, and wisdom and generous support on the other.

Wa kuume haukati wa kushoto
THE RIGHT HAND DOES NOT CUT OFF THE LEFT HAND

For all the disagreements and differences, a family bond is one of the greatest phenomena of all time.

Kila shina lina incha
EVERY ROOT HAS ITS END

A deep sense of insecurity and anguish amongst any community is contagious and damaging. Similarly, families that have experienced trauma in one generation, usually, unknowingly and unwittingly, pass it on to the next generation. It can be stopped. Intergenerational trauma is a condition that continues to gain recognition. There are ways of dealing with it. Identifying and acknowledging the disruptive events that destabilised the family unit is an important first step. Seeking professional help such as counselling is crucial. Break the cycle.

Asiyesikia la mkuu huvunjika guu

ONE THAT DOES NOT HEED ADVICE BREAKS A LEG

Not all advice is good advice. Not all advice is bad advice. Listen, digest, trust your gut, just don't ignore it.

Chungu wa mwana aujuae mzazi

A PARENT KNOWS THEIR CHILD'S STRUGGLES

The welfare of the people you love is just as important as your own. The impact from the inability to help alleviate issues which affect family members can be damaging and detrimental to one's health. Be kind to yourself and keep up with a job well done by your loving presence and unconditional love. Carers within households are the unseen and unsung heroes of today. Listen and support them, don't judge.

Asiyefunzwa na mamaye ufunzwa na ulimwengu

WHOEVER FAILS TO LEARN FROM THEIR MOTHER IS TAUGHT BY THE WORLD

A parent's love is protective. Do listen to the advice of someone who not only knows you well but means well and has more life experience than you. Such honest insight is rare, so let loose rigid opinions and remain open to new suggestions. Of course, you may choose to ignore all advice and instead opt to learn your own long, bitter and hard way.

Chapter 5

ON TOGETHERNESS — UJAMAA

Mtu ni watu

A PERSON IS PEOPLE

A person is singular and incomplete until completed by the plurality of other people. Consider this - just as a garden's beauty flows from all its flora and fauna, a person's well-being is derived from togetherness. The concept of *ujamaa* in Swahili means familyhood based on solidarity founded in traditional African society. 'We are all in it together, socially and economically'. With changing times, this concept has evolved but the message remains as relevant. Your success springs from collaborating with others. Take note: an act of kindness is only but another blessing waiting to happen to you.

Kinyozi hajinyoi

A BARBER DOES NOT SHAVE HIMSELF

'Stand on your own two feet, be self-sufficient' does not mean that you go at it alone. Consider your life's goals like you would a tournament. The top league sportsmen and women understand that no game is won by a single player.

Panapo wengi hapaharibiki neno

WHERE THERE ARE MANY THERE ARE NO OBSTACLES

Don't allow past experiences of being let down cloud your judgement and hinder your ability to build new relationships. The value of team work cannot be underestimated. Pulling diverse skills and different perspectives results in solutions and reduces a heavy workload.

Udugu wa nazi mkutano pakachani

THERE IS NO BROTHERHOOD IN COCONUTS UNLESS IN THE COOKING POT

When things are going well, take the time to reach out and mend those relationships that you may have been neglecting. Don't leave it too long, circumstances change and not always for the better.

Kidole kimoja hakivunji chawa

ONE FINGER DOES NOT CRUSH LICE

Invest in restoring family relationships and building friendships. Make connections by being generous with your time and celebrating others' achievements. When issues arise as they sometimes do, a little help from those who care about you, will go a long way.

Tulia tuishi wazuri hawaishi

LET'S SETTLE DOWN, ATTRACTIVE PEOPLE ARE PLENTIFUL

A happy union demands the recognition that other potential matches will continue to exist. Romance may begin with feelings, but to last, love demands a commitment and meeting of minds.

Mtu pweke ni uvundo

A LONE PERSON IS LIKE A FOUL ODOUR

This is a shout-out to all you lone rangers – you are so cool! The bad news is that everyone remains suspicious of you.

Nguzo moja haijengi nyumba

ONE WALL DOES NOT BUILD A HOUSE

As much as you would like to view yourself as self-reliant, it is only by combining your efforts with others that you gain the best results.

Dunia Duara
THE WORLD IS ROUND
Right back at ya! Whatever you do comes back to either haunt or reward you. Choose carefully. 😊

Jicho haliwezi kujiona
AN EYE CANNOT SEE ITSELF
Ants build castles by clubbing together and helping each other out. Drawing strength in numbers. The next time you take on a task, think of an ant.

Furaha hukolea mkiwa wengi
HAPPINESS MULTIPLIES WHEN SHARED
Wait, happiness?! Who has it and where did they get it from? Go on, throw us a party. 🥳

Jamala yako haipotei
KINDNESS IS NOT LOST
Kindness creates a ripple that just keeps spreading in gigantic circles. It is bound to come back to you. Add to this the other rewards of warmth and joy you will experience every time your halo lights up from giving.

Rehema, kisima

COMPASSION IS LIKE A WELL

Not everyone looks forward to birthdays or countdowns to anniversaries. Not everyone longs for the new burst of spring flowers or the first rays of the summer sun. Not everyone is eager for Christmas or Thanksgiving. Not everyone yearns to get home. With everyone you meet, be nice, it doesn't cost you anything, but it may mean the world to them.

Chapter 6

ON SPENDING, SAVING AND ALL THAT

Akiba haiozi

SAVINGS DO NOT ROT

Eat, drink and be merry, but not all at once. Excess equals waste. Good times do come to an end.

Kukopa arusi kulipa matanga

BORROWING IS A WEDDING, PAYING BACK IS A FUNERAL

Putting off money issues for another day is not resolving the issue. Don't kid yourself.

Afya bora kuliko mali

HEALTH IS GREATER THAN WEALTH

Not being able to pay bills or sustain a decent living is miserable and demeaning. There are no volunteers for that stress club. However, how far and how long you choose to sacrifice health in pursuit of wealth is a question each and every person should know the answer to.

Adha huzua karadha
HARDSHIP BEGETS DEBT

Just own it. As far as possible, accept the austerity that comes from being broke and by doing so, you will be able to take the next step on the road to finding long-lasting solutions. Keep borrowing and you will keep digging yourself into a hole. Always remember, in good times anticipate the bad times and in bad times anticipate the good times.

Mali ya urithi haina baraka
INHERITED WEALTH HAS NO BLESSING

Often little or no contribution has been made for the spoils and yet families are torn apart over what was meant to be shared. Dig for your own treasure.

Mali ni sawa na maua
RICHES ARE LIKE FLOWERS

Money in the bank? Here today, gone tomorrow.

Mali ya kumtia mwenyewe utumwani si mali
WEALTH THAT ENSLAVES YOU IS NOT WEALTH

Wealth is not well-being. Well-being is wealth. Define what wealth means to you, then draw a line and stand by the choices you make.

Cha mjinga huzama cha mwerevu huelea
A FOOL'S VESSEL SINKS, A WISEMAN'S VESSEL FLOATS

New media adores affluence; wealth; glamour; luxury; indulgence; opulence and so on. There's nothing wrong with trying to join the happy shiny people. First though, find what makes *you* happy.

Haba na haba hujaza kibaba
DROP BY DROP FILLS THE JUG

Seeds planted today may take several seasons to grow. Do, link up a savings plan to your earnings. Don't, ignore debt, take the emotional aspects out of the situation by finding practical repayment solutions. Be patient and keep sowing.

Mtumai cha ndugu hufa yu ali maskani
HE WHO RELIES ON THE KINDNESS OF OTHERS DIES A PAUPER

At times it's a marathon and other times

it's the 100-metres singles. The world is an intricate unfair system. It is complicated for Global South countries too. On the one hand, trying to shake off the exploitative colonial legacies, whilst trying to develop good governance and build stable economies on the other. Meanwhile the youth climb over borders in search for survival. What then? There are no easy solutions. Self-reliance without backup is a fallacy. Be selective, with and from whom you seek help, take charge of your destiny. Learn from the success of those who have overcome similar barriers and adapt their winning strategies to your plan of action.

Mali ni nganzi, utakapo hupanda
RICHES ARE LIKE A LADDER, TO ATTAIN THEM ONE MUST CLIMB

To achieve success as an entrepreneur, in gainful employment, sport, as an artist or in so called passive income gigs - in whatever field of your choosing; it all begins with dedication, self-belief and hard bl***y work.

Ishi uwezavyo si upendavyo
LIVE ACCORDING TO YOUR MEANS, NOT YOUR DESIRES

Spend with aspiration in mind, not with desperation. Budget for everything. Do not allow passing emotions obscure your judgement. Wait patiently for success' grand arrival.

Nyumba ya njuni, haioni nduni
A BIRD IS NOT ASHAMED OF ITS NEST

Poverty is degrading. The inability to support one's family breaks the human spirit. This lack of means may at times attract contempt from narrow-minded people. Ignore them. Be proud of what you have overcome so far. Luckily, most sensible people are too pre-occupied with their own worries to give yours a second thought.

Juhudi si kupata, kupata ni majaliwa
EFFORT IS NOT AS TO PROSPERITY AS PROSPERITY IS TO BLESSINGS

It is a false start! There are those that are born beyond the finishing line. Yes, but nobility comes from getting up every morning with the goal and determination to work hard to provide for one's family. Quite rightly so.

Mzika pembe ndiye mzua pembe
HE WHO BURIES TREASURE UNEARTHS TREASURE

Invest in yourself. Avoid being a cookie-profiled news junkie. Your interests today should not shape your newsfeed forever. Read widely. If you are able to, travel. Change your scenery and pursue new experiences that will quieten your inner monologue and in turn reduce stress. Study or sign up for free courses. If time allows, volunteer.

Chapter 7

ON RANDOM BUT IMPORTANT LESSONS

Lisilokuwapo moyoni, halipo machoni
ITS ONLY VISIBLE WHEN IT COMES FROM THE HEART

It is only through your imagination that you can envision your destination. A feigned desire will not be achieved no matter how grand or appealing. A simple sincere wish is more likely to come true long after it has been forgotten. Take the time to know yourself. You can only go as far as your mind's eye can see.

Kikulacho kii nguoni mwako
WHATEVER BITES YOU DWELLS IN YOUR CLOTHING

You can predict, with some precision, future pitfalls by being brutally honest with yourself about your shortcomings. You may view yourself as successfully functioning, borderline functioning or totally dysfunctional. These are all shades of normality. Don't suffer in silence if you find yourself unable to cope. Search for professional help and speak to someone. You are not alone.

Pilipili usiyo ila, yakuashia nini?
WHY DOES ANOTHER PERSON EATING CHILLI PEPPER BURN YOUR MOUTH?

Mind your own business.

Kitanda usichokilalia hujui kunguni chake
FOR A BED YOU DO NOT LIE IN YOU DO NOT KNOW OF ITS BUGS

Other people's lives appear amazing from a distance. Many a time, all sorts of strain and emotional drama is hidden beneath the smiles. Instagram is one moment amongst many other unseen moments.

Adui mpende
LOVE YOUR ENEMY

When Nelson Mandela was interviewed about his feelings regarding revenge and human appetite for satisfaction, he said, 'It is not easy, when you are busy with constructive work to think about issues that make you bitter. Bitterness comes easily when one is idle with nothing to do. If you are engaged with something positive, constructive and rewarding you are likely to forget experiences which have been counterproductive.' – CBC News, Barbara Frum's interview with Nelson Mandela.

Chui naye ana mkwewe
A LEOPARD HAS A MOTHER-IN-LAW

Each villain has a figure they respect as well as a cheering squad… Don't ask.

Muingereza hutengeza akakereza
THE COLONIALIST BUILDS TO DESTROY

The slave trade of people from Africa which lasted for at least 300 years was legally abolished in the UK by the Slavery Abolition Act(s) of 1 May 1807 and 1 August 1834; in the USA, the Emancipation Proclamation was issued on 1 January 1863. The plot continued. Some eighty years later, on 26 February 1885, after the transatlantic slave trade was first abolished, Africa was officially carved up for occupation and exploitation for another 100 years until as late as 1980, officially. Unofficially, it is far worse. The effects of centuries of dehumanising legacies of a population for commercial profit are complex and include ongoing global social prejudice, chronic economic under development and inter-generation trauma, which will reverberate for years to come. The truth is yet to be told.

Mtego bila chambo haunusi
A TRAP WITHOUT BAIT IS USELESS

Minimum effort with maximum gain is a thing. Seriously, google it. Or just stop procrastinating and give whatever you do, your very best shot.

Ahera si mbali kwa mwenye maisha
THE AFTERLIFE IS NEVER FAR AWAY TO THOSE LIVING

No amount of rationalism can explain the fragility of life. For those that have sadly encountered traumatic bereavement, the loss is numbing and the pain, debilitating. Life divides into before and after sequels. Loneliness descends as the everyday joyful moments disappear. Prayer consoles. Talking soothes. Time heals. Be kind to yourself.

Kweli iliyo chungu si uwongo mtamu
THE BITTER TRUTH IS NOT A SWEET LIE

These days, you can be *cancelled* faster than you can say Ha*Kuna Matata*. Everyone is about to be offended.

History is selectively based on dimmed viewpoints. A denial of uncomfortable events is the norm. Debate has been replaced with partisan, polarised opinions. Facts are optional. When truth is the dare, it's no longer a game.

Kulenga si kufuma
TO AIM IS NOT TO SHOOT

At least I tried is not an achievement. The habit of half-hearted efforts results in a pattern of unfinished projects and unrealised potential. A failed attempt should not be viewed as a consolation trophy.

Liandikwalo ndiyo liwalo
A WRITTEN ACCOUNT BECOMES THE VERIFIED ACCOUNT

To preserve the truth, history and culture, there must be a written account of it. Yet preserving African and Indigenous cultures and languages around the world comes on the heels of competing economic development initiatives, efforts to eradicate poverty and in some regions, raging civil conflict. Will there be any room left for introspection or retrospection?

Kuishi kwingi ni kuona mengi
A LONG LIFE SEES A GREAT DEAL

The bad news is that learning from older generations has been eclipsed by echo chambers that is modern technology. The good news is that technology is also filled with ample content such as, informative podcasts or interviews of successful people as well as insightful lectures. Do yourself a favour, learn from those that have walked a mile or two.

Mpika vyungu viwili, kimoja huunguwa
ONE WHO COOKS TWO POTS WILL BURN ONE

There is a time for everything makes perfect sense to some people. For the ADHD brain, every time is for everything. Educate yourself and others on how your physical or neurodevelopmental condition may be affecting your thinking patterns and moderate your behaviour patterns to deal with it.

Asiyekujua hakuthamini
A STRANGER IS NOT RECOGNISED

Build up your network. Being introduced works better than arriving out of the blue.

Ndege mjanja hunaswa na tunda bovu

A CUNNING BIRD IS TRAPPED BY OVERRIPE FRUIT

Think you are above all temptation? Think again.

Ujana moshi, uzee kutu

YOUTH IS TO SMOKE AS OLD AGE IS TO RUST

To anyone under the age of 20, everyone over 40 is old and quite frankly should have planned their life better. As they say, don't judge a book by its cover - life does not usually go according to plan. Straight roads meander. Years fly past. Make the most of your time whatever your age.

Hotuba in fedha, kimya in dhahabu

SPEECH IS SILVER, SILENCE IS GOLD

It's your call.

Shibe ya hasidi ni majuto

THE REWARD FOR THE PURSUIT OF A GRUDGE IS REGRET

There are 24 hours in a day. Within those 24 hours, how is it that you can possibly find time to think about anything that does not benefit you?

IS IT DAWN, IS IT DAWN? IT HAS DAWNED

The idea that that some countries are on the road to going from under-developed to developing, then to emerging, after which they become a fully-fledged but 'struggling economy' and finally, one fine day, to global players, is stuff for academics to ponder, whilst everyone else works their socks off. You will be hard pressed to find a youth in Africa today who attributes their plight to the centuries of exploitation by the West. Instead, they are more likely to point at the misuse of public funds in the last three decades by their elected leaders. Après-colonial exploitation and post-colonial corruption are sisters. If these sisters are eradicated, will African nations keep marching on the same spot? Change is coming. The decades that follow will tell. The upcoming crop of young leaders may well propel this abundantly resourced continent, above the heights and awe of its snow-capped mountains.

A word of caution – book that safari today. For if prosperity means closed borders (as it evidently does), an entry visa to catch a glimpse of the big five may soon be worth its weight in gold.

Chapter 8

ON THE ART OF BEING CIVILISED

Mwungwana ni kitendo

A CIVILISED PERSON IS KNOWN BY HIS ACTIONS

The Swahili word for civilised is *ungwana*. It means having the highest regard for other people. That includes how a person treats his or her parents, the elderly neighbour, the disadvantaged, as well as the respect and courtesy he or she affords others and their property. It is not about six-course dinners. Therein lies the beauty in every culture.

Afuataye upepo huenda uendako

WHOEVER FOLLOWS THE WIND ENDS UP WHEREVER IT BLOWS

This is for you if you are waiting in the shadows for a champion to emerge so you can align yourself with them. If you are not open to discussion and are involved in culture wars of absolutes:

sinner, saint, right, left, woke, anti-woke, them, us, finger-wagging, privileged backlashing, Orwellian witch-hunts. The world's temperatures are rising, conflicts are raging. History is repeating itself. The only moral high ground is peaceful co-existence. Go on, get your T-shirt branded: I.

Mume ni jaha, si raha
A MAN'S THRONE IS EARNED
Poem
'Modern man'
Oh, modern man
To abide by your wishes
And stop your mutterings
I hereby declare
Every storm cancelled
Every raindrop dried
Every lightning stopped
Every wind gale stilled
At your convenience,
Oh, modern man

Fuata hekima upate heshima
PURSUE INTEGRITY TO GAIN RESPECT
Whatever this means to you today, give yourself the permission to change your mind as you grow older and wiser.

Mwenye shoka hakosi kuni
THE OWNER OF AN AXE DOES NOT LACK FIREWOOD

Invest your time in developing a skill or gaining a qualification. It will be the gift that keeps on giving to your future self.

Simba angurumaye si mwindaji
A ROARING LION IS NOT A HUNTING LION

Getting things done is more important than trying to gain attention. Just show up and keep at it. As soon as the opportunity presents itself, you will be perfectly aligned and prepared to take advantage.

Mambo taratibu humshinda mwenye nguvu
STRENGTH IS NO MATCH FOR DILIGENCE

In martial arts, training is based on discipline, self-control and perseverance, and yet when applied in combat, these elements can be lethal. Apply yourself consistently, and progression will follow from a steady accumulation of effort.

Kufa kufaana
DEATH, THE EQUALISER

All men are created equal. Privileges and opportunities may dictate access to pearls and diamonds, yet we all share the fragility and fate that is every living creature.

Akomelepo mwenyeji na mgeni koma hapo
A GUEST IMITATES THE HOST

Dishing out well-meaning advice is just as unwelcome as receiving unsolicited directions. Unless asked, keep your opinions to yourself.

Akumulikaye mchana usiku atakuchoma
HE WHO SHINES A LIGHT AT YOU DURING THE DAY WILL BURN YOU AT NIGHT

Remain wary of people who flatter you. Distance yourself from sly, two-faced characters. The wisdom from Maya Angelou says it all: 'When someone shows you who they are, believe them the first time'.

Ukidharau chako utaiba
IF YOU DESPISE YOURSELF YOU WILL END UP STEALING FROM OTHERS

Embrace who and where you find yourself. Honour those that have paid the price for today's freedoms. Show gratitude for the heroes; because of their sacrifice and courage, you stand tall, you dream, you are seen.

Mtu hajisifu bali husifiwa na wengine

A PERSON DOES NOT PRAISE HIMSELF, HE IS PRAISED BY OTHERS

Social media is a self-promotion parade. Surely everybody knows that? 😏

Mwenye roho ya furaha huzudia raha

ONE WITH A CHEERFUL HEART FINDS JOY IN LITTLE THINGS

Somewhere between being born and growing up the difference between the haves and the have-nots becomes crystal clear. The pursuit to leave one camp, join the other camp and remain in nice camp becomes lifelong. This natural pursuit should not distort your own personal definition of happiness. On the days that you find contentment, you have achieved serenity, be grateful. Nature is the best teacher on the importance of balance. The effects of imbalance on the world's ecosystem are obvious. The message is balance and it is yet to reach mankind on planet Earth.

Hasiri hasara

ANGER, LOSS

Calm down. Seriously!

Ukienda kwa mwenye chongo fumba lako jicho

WHEN VISITING A ONE-EYED PERSON, CLOSE ONE EYE TOO

The ability to understand another's point of view is the starting point for any successful negotiation.

Akili ni mali

INTELLIGENCE IS WEALTH

Make good use of your natural talents, the robots are coming.

Asiyejua utu si mtu

A PERSON WITHOUT MANNERS IS NOT A PERSON

Being polite is one of the easiest ways to influence people. Your bias, both conscious and unconscious, is borne out of your life experiences. Learning to identify and overcome your own biases will be your secret weapon to getting things done.

Ukidharau chako utaiba

IF YOU DO NOT APPRECIATE YOUR ROOTS, YOU WILL FIND YOURSELF SPONGING OFF OTHERS

Indigenous cultures around the world, stand up and be counted. Your ancestors lived on the land, from the land and for the land. Distinguished in their knowledge of plants that heal and potions that soothe. Advanced in their understanding of the fragility of the eco-system. Well-versed in the time-honoured practices of balancing give and take. Skilled at building castles from the earth and with the earth. Generous to strangers and welcoming to many a weary traveller. As Bob Marley sang, 'None but ourselves can free our mind'.

For more details visit:
https://whc.unesco.org/en/list

Chapter 9

ON GENEROSITY

Kutoa ni moyo usambe ni utajiri
CHARITY COMES FROM THE HEART, NOT WEALTH

The World Giving Index measures giving in three ways: helping a stranger; donating money; or volunteering. Annual compiled data shows a number of countries scoring high on aggregate generosity, despite experiencing severe economic issues and comparatively low happiness levels.

Report by Charities Aid Foundation [see table in resources].

Rahisi huvunja upishi
CHEAPNESS SPOILS GOOD COOKING

Shortcuts take longer than the so-called longer way. Always strive to earn it, not grab it. This applies in business too. Conglomerate firms have taken over the mantle from the colonisers. The scramble for minerals in Africa continues. Whole villages are bulldozed and habitants displaced for mining, whilst debt bonds and the promise of kickbacks keep the host governments in check. In the firms' home countries, dividends, profits and taxes keep everyone in ha ha land. The next time you charge your phone, or ride in your eco-friendly electric car, spare a thought for the artisan (a.k.a. hands to pick axe) cobalt miners in countries such as the Democratic Republic of Congo. There in the darkest state of inhumane drudgery, your shiny new gadgets keep lighting up.

Chapter 10

ON BEING HAKUNA MATATA

Nguvu in maarifa
KNOWLEDGE IS STRENGTH

To limit yourself to the confines of your imagination is one thing, to limit yourself to the confines of somebody else's view of who and what you ought to be is practically a *sin*. Do not be intimidated by the accomplishments of others; they too had to learn. Let your curiosity lead you. Empower your journey by choosing to be a lifelong student.

Maneno ni daraja, hayazuii maji kuteremka
GOSSIP IS LIKE WATER UNDER A BRIDGE

Let them talk!

Elfu huanzia moja
ONE THOUSAND STARTS WITH ONE

Start somewhere, however small and

celebrate the small triumphs. Do treat every win with caution. It is easy to spend it all without realising, because it seems too little to generate any savings or it seems so much that it appears infinite.

Raha haina kahara
HAPPINESS HAS NO BLEMISH

Cheer up, smile, let your heart sing: for on the day that the sun shines on you, there shall not be a single speck of cloud in the wide, blue sky.

Tajiri ni yule asiye na mahitaji mengi
A RICH PERSON IS ONE WITH FEW DESIRES

This is how to be *Hakuna Matata*. Taking the time to find the small joys in today, whilst looking into the future with hope and purpose. Despite outward perceptions, material wealth does not provide insulation from anxiety or depression. Healing comes from finding the equilibrium within oneself. A happy life is a journey not a destination.

Dunia ni darubini
THE WORLD IS LIKE A PAIR OF BINOCULARS

It is not so much the things that you do (as presumably you have made your peace with these), it's the things that you don't do and should do, that you need worry about. Simply put, strive to do the right thing.

Dhahabu haina maana ndani ya ardhi
GOLD HAS NO VALUE UNDERNEATH THE GROUND
Possessing talent is not enough. You will need to be prepared to roll up your sleeves, muck in the murk, push and be shoved, fail and almost fade before, if you are lucky, you get noticed. It's all worth it, though.

Ajabu ya kondoo kucheka kioo
THE IRONY OF A SHEEP LAUGHING IN THE MIRROR
Well done, you, for making the right choices and achieving your dreams, unlike those who obviously have not worked hard enough! Right? Wrong. Each and every person in the world strives for love, security and well-being. Most people are just as smart and have put in more time and effort than you. Get off your high horse.

Cha kunvunja hakina rubani
A FAULTY SHIP WILL SINK DESPITE ITS CAPTAIN
How fit are you? Not just squats and planks but also mentally and spiritually.

All three aspects of well-being are equally important. Taking up exercise improves both physical and mental health. Mental health can also be greatly improved by talking. Find a safe environment to share your thoughts or attend individual counselling. Whatever your religious views may be, spiritual growth derives from a desire to know more about God or to explore the meaning of faith. The basics for Christian faith are love, love, love. And it's not easy. The rewards include inner peace. Take charge of you.

Mvua hainyeshei mmoja
RAIN DOES NOT FALL ON ONE PERSON

Look around you, and even when you don't see it, know that suffering is universal.

Enenda na ulionalo
CARRY ON AS OTHERS DO

Sometimes the best advice is simply to observe, learn and imitate.

La anasa bure halipatikani
THE EASY WAY OUT IS NOWHERE TO BE FOUND

Time for action. What are you willing to sacrifice to pursue your dreams? If enduring ridiculous amounts of work, side hustling, rehearsals and rejections, etcetera, for the promise of a less than certain future reward – is not your style, think again.

Hapana bahari bila mawimbi
EVERY SEA HAS ITS WAVES

Although some challenges are foreseeable, life may throw a few curveballs along the way. When these arise, remember all you need do is take, each day at a time. Tackle the unfolding fear with faith whilst you gradually adjust your settings from default mode to new mode. Take heart, every storm shall pass.

Chuki hupotoa watu
HATE RUINS HUMANITY

Credit where credit is due. Whereas racial discrimination a few decades ago was legal and enforced in most countries around the world, discrimination based on race and other characteristics, today is unlawful or is gradually being phased out. This is some progress for institutional prejudicial oppression but has not been sufficient progress in the safeguard of precious lives[*]. Despite these failures, backlash backed by collective amnesia awaits the notion that 'Black people', not to mention, 'Black lives' or 'diversity in institutions' matters. A short lens view reveals a mixture of fear and insecurity breeding resentment and contempt. Other prevailing complexities demand expertise beyond the research capabilities of this little book. On the flipside, it is important to note that the majority of folks from all walks of life, continue to work tirelessly to uphold social justice, end discrimination and fight for equal access to opportunities, for peace, for unity, for *hakuna matata* love.

PS: *Hakuna matata* is not ignorance, nor is it wilful blindness, rather it is a conscious decision to choose to spread kindness, love and joy to whomever happens to come your way, today.

---

[*] The murder of George Perry Floyd Jr., by police officers in 2020, shocked the world and prompted global protests. The record of names of unarmed African-Americans killed by law enforcement officers in the United States dates back from 1800s. Unfortunately, victims continue to be added to the list to this day.

Ujamaa haukusanywi hugaiwa
BROTHERHOOD IS NOT AN ASSEMBLY; IT IS SHARING

The reluctance to give often originates from the conviction that there is not enough for oneself let alone others. If the world over were truly committed to the eradication of the indignity of poverty within and outside national borders, credible steps would be implemented to make it happen. Space exploration is cool but so are technology and infrastructure projects on Earth.

Ni asili ya binadamu kutotosheka
IT IS IN THE NATURE OF MANKIND TO NEVER BE SATISFIED

It's one thing to pursue your dreams, it's another thing to fail to recognise that new desires will always be waiting by the wings. Take a break, enjoy the harvest.

Furaha ina hitaji cha kufanya, cha kupenda na cha kutamaini.
HAPPINESS THRIVES ON SOMETHING TO DO, SOMETHING TO LOVE, AND SOMETHING TO HOPE FOR.

Full stop.

EPILOGUE

Kweli ukidhihiri uwongo hujitenga
WHEN TRUTH ARRIVES, FALSEHOODS MUST GIVE WAY

Declaration on the Right to Development
– United Nations General Assembly 1986

Art. 1. 'The right to development is an inalienable human right by virtue of which every human person and all peoples are entitled to participate in, contribute to, and enjoy economic, social, cultural and political development, in which all human rights and fundamental freedoms can be fully realized'.

Acknowledgements

First and foremost, to the *Wahenga* – the wise old men and women who devised these *methali*. The world may not know your names, but your wit, wisdom, insight, poetry and philosophy, lives on, and will continue to do so for many generations to come. *Asanteni sana.*

Second, I owe a world of gratitude to my family for their patience and support. For your gentle and not-so-gentle critiquing that shaped my ramblings into some sort of coherent text. Without you, this little book would have remained at the bottom of the pile of my never-ending to-do list. Thanks for being truly *Hakuna Matata* with me.

Last and most sincerely, I am grateful for God's Divine Mercy. But for your Grace, oh Lord.

Resources

Escrivá, Josemari, *The Way, The Essential Classic of Opus Dei Founder*
Wamitila, K.W., *Kamusi ya Methali*
The Holy Bible – Scripture References
Niebuhr, Reinhold – Author and Theologian
Kara, Siddharth, *How the Blood of the Congo Powers Our Lives*

Suggested Reading[**]
https://sdgs.un.org – Follow, like, share: @sdgaction
https://raid-uk.org - Follow, like, share: @raidukorg

[**] The author is not affiliated, associated, authorised, endorsed by, or in any way officially connected with any of the organisations mentioned in this book. The views, thoughts, and opinions expressed in this book belong solely to the author, and do not represent the views of any organisation.

https://whc.unesco.org/en/list
https://www.cafonline.org
https://worldhappiness.report
http://undocs.org/A/HRC/54/27
https://www.bbc.com/swahili

Mental Health resources[***]
Region: USA
Call or text the National Suicide Prevention
Lifeline on 988, chat on 988lifeline.org, or
text HOME to 741741 to connect with a crisis
counsellor.

Other sources of helpline hotlines:
(findahelpline.com)
Other helpline resources can be found at: https://
www.obama.org/programs/my-brothers-keeper-
alliance/events/town-halls/mental-health-
communities-color/

[***] This list of mental-health resource websites is provided
for information purposes only. Inclusion on the list
does not amount to a recommendation nor is it an
endorsement of any of the organisations on the list.
The author bears no responsibility for the accuracy or
legality of the content of the sites or subsequent links
from any website cited on this page.

Region: UK
Samaritans can be contacted on freephone
116 123, or email jo@samaritans.org or jo@
samaritans.ie.
Other helpline resources can be found at: Service
Directory | Campaign Against Living Miserably
(CALM) (thecalmzone.net)

Region: International
International helplines can be found at:
befrienders.org
https://twloha.com/find-help/international-
resources/

Table: Compares the top 20 World Giving rankings against country's GDP and Happiness Index

No.	World Giving Index 2023: Top 20 countries Ranking	Country GDP (Nominal) per Capita Index 2022: Ranking	World Happiness Report 2022: Ranking
1	Indonesia	113	84
2	Ukraine	114	92
3	Kenya	149	111
4	Liberia	179	125
5	United States of America	7	15
6	Myanmar	168	117
7	Kuwait	32	No data
8	Canada	17	13
9	Nigeria	39	95
10	New Zealand	151	10
11	United Arab Emirates	20	26
12	Gambia	176	119
13	Denmark	9	2
14	Australia	10	12
15	Northen Cyprus	31	46
16	Ethiopia	170	124
17	Ireland	2	14
18	United Kingdom	22	19
19	Norway	3	7
20	Malta	28	37

Sources: Charities aid foundation: https://www.cafonline.org; The World Happiness Report a partnership of Gallup, the Oxford Wellbeing Research Centre, the UN Sustainable Development Solutions Network, and the WHR's Editorial Board: https://worldhappiness.report and The World Bank: https://www.worldbank.org/en/home

FUN FACTS ABOUT SWAHILI

❀

Swahili, also known as *Kiswahili*, is a Bantu language. It is also derived from Arabic, Portuguese and Latin vocabulary as it emerged as the prominent trading language along the coastal shores of Eastern Africa.

❀

The number of Swahili speakers globally is estimated at 50–150 million.

❀

Google provides a Google Kiswahili – search/ translate/glosbe

❀

Swahili is spoken in the following countries as an official language: Kenya; Tanzania; Zanzibar; and Uganda. As a national language in: Rwanda, Burundi, Malawi, Zambia, Mozambique and the

Democratic Republic of Congo. Comoros Island and Madagascar also speak dialects of Swahili. South Africa introduced Swahili as an option in its school curriculum from 2020.

❀

The following universities offer Swahili language as an option: University of London (SoaS); Colombia University; Cornell University; University of Gothenburg; University of Queensland; University of Edinburgh; University of Pennsylvania; University of Pittsburgh; Northwestern University; Ohio University; University of Mississippi; Boston University; University of North Carolina; University of Chicago and University of Washington, University of Georgetown, University of Wisconsin, amongst others.

❀

The BBC World Service broadcasts world news in Swahili [https://www.bbc.com/swahili].

❀

Radio Deutsche Welle (Köln, Germany) broadcasts world news in Swahili for radio broadcasts.

❀

Habari za UN is the United Nations dedicated news site in Swahili.

This book is printed on paper from sustainable sources managed under the Forest Stewardship Council (FSC) scheme.

It has been printed in the UK to reduce transportation miles and their impact upon the environment.

For every new title that Troubador publishes, we plant a tree to offset CO_2, partnering with the More Trees scheme.

MORE TREES
LET'S PLANT A BILLION TREES

For more about how Troubador offsets its environmental impact, see www.troubador.co.uk/sustainability-and-community